COCKTAIL BOOK

The Ultimate Cocktail Recipe Book with 200 Cocktails

EDEN BROWN

Copyright © 2017

All rights reserved. No part of this book may be reproduced or transmitted in any form or by any electronic or mechanical means, including photocopy, recording, or any information storage and retrieval system now known or to be invented, without written permission from the author, except by a reviewer who wishes to quote brief passages in connection with a review written for inclusion in a magazine, newspaper, website, or broadcast.

Disclaimer: Neither the author nor the publisher shall be held liable or responsible to any person or entity with respect to any loss or incidental or consequential damages caused, directly or indirectly, by the information or programs contained herein. You must seek the services of a competent professional before beginning any health or weight-loss advice. References are provided for informational purposes only. They do not constitute endorsement of any websites or other sources.

CONTENTS

Green Island 13

Last Rainbow 14

Maraboo 15

Sweet Chocolate 16

Umbrella 17

Blue Sky 18

Lady in Pink 19

Kiss on the Lips 20

Vodkaland 21

Watermelon Kiss 22

Zombie 23

The Last Sunset 24

The Alligator 25

Sea Waters 26

Vodka Schnapps 27

Madrid 28

Purple Poison 29

Coconut Island 30

Monkey's Booze 31

La Mariposa 32

Antman 33

La Passion 34

Captain Jack 35

Lucy 36

Sunshine 37

Dark Captain 38

Magician 39

Mango Mania	40
Monday	41
Gambit	42
Summer days	43
Bitter Love	44
Fast & Furious	45
Zeus	46
Empty Island	47
Cool Kid	48
Coke Rum	49
Green Poison	50
LianYu	51
Banana Rum	52
The Beast	53
Genius	54
Black Canary	55
The Man	56
Samba	57
The Big Bang	58
Lost	59
Tropico	60
The Secret Alley	61
The Bear	62
Duty Free	63
Lost Pirate	64
Friday the 13th	65
Dark Summer Night	66
Forestberry	67
Camping Gin	68

Gringo	69
Creamy Gin	70
Apricot Love Potion	71
Sugar Mama	72
Mariachi	73
Industrial	74
Dragonfly	75
Texas Rangers	76
Insideus	77
Sexy Margarita	78
Peachy Tequila	79
Uptown	80
La Manche	81
Apple Tequila	82
Lost Captain Jack	83
Rimini	84
Don Agosto	85
The more the better	86
Margarita Island	87
Mexican Waters	88
Mayan Secret	89
Cancun Moonlight	90
Cocktail Del Carmen	91
Night in Acapulco	92
Spring Vacation	93
Perl of Harbor	94
Maroon 5	95
Cocktail Pie	96
Banana Daiquiri	97

Kiwi cream martini	98
Frozen Yogurt	99
Cold Pear	100
SnowWhite	101
Mango Spiced	102
Speedy Gonzales	103
Poirot	104
Incadescent	105
Shadowspire	106
Summer in Greece	107
Sidari Sunshine	108
Hide and Seek	109
Hypnotiser	110
Fiji	111
Adventures	112
The Real Godfather	113
Don Juan	114
New York's Mystery Lady	115
Jack's Special	116
LadyBug	117
Watermelon Whiskey	118
Frozen Whiskey Time	119
Summer Whiskey	120
Whiskey Lemonade	121
Apple Bourbon	122
Amaretto Whiskey	123
Whiskey Sleeping Pill	124
Mint Whiskey	125
Rainstorm	126

Sweet Gentleman	127
Brown Whiskey	128
Sweet Fruity Whiskey	129
Banana Whiskey	130
Caramel Whiskey	131
Spring Breeze	132
Red Russian	133
Big Foot	134
Santorini Paradise	135
Moscato	136
White Magic	137
Drunk	138
F.R.I.E.N.D.S	139
Blueberry Sauvignon	140
Bloody Wine	141
Citrus Garden	142
Green Lemonade	143
Roselyn	144
Bad Blood	145
Peach Wine	146
Red & Yellow	147
Submarine	148
Paradise Nectar	149
Thunder Cry	150
Falling Sky	151
The Passenger	152
Paradise Lost	153
Atlanta City	154
Karma	155

Devious Lady	156
Sensai	157
Strange man in the rain	158
Pear Flavored Beer	159
Dark Passenger's Drink	160
Troublemaker	161
Shadow Ally	162
Summer in Brazil	163
King of Jungle	164
99 Nights	165
Rendez-Vouz	166
Walking on the Sun	167
Mi casa estu casa	168
Tequila Beer	169
Ginger Beer	170
Fruity Beer	171
Parachute Pass	172
Italian Sunset	173
Peachy Champagne Cocktail	174
Fruity Champagne	175
Fancy Champagne Lady	176
The Weekend	177
Strawberry Champagne	178
Vodka Champagne	179
Sweet Champagne Water	180
Red Elegance	181
Cakey Champagne	182
Blue Champagne	183
Purple Mermaid	184

Hypnotic	185
Red Bull Champagne	186
Bittersweet Champagne	187
Moi & Toi	188
Afternoon in Hawaii	189
Fresh Lavender	190
Delux Champagne	191
Cherry Pie Champagne	192
Lady Brandy Cocktail	193
Metropolitan Cocktail	194
Adventurous	195
Peach Brandy	196
Refreshing Raspberry Cocktail	197
Navy Cocktail	198
Apple Brandy	199
Hot and Cold	200
Ying and Yang	201
Headache	202
Clear Sky	203
Cranberry Brandy	204
Red Brandy	205
Sparkling Brandy	206
Delicious Mix	207
Sugarish Brandy	208
Tropical Island	209
Summertime Sadness	210
Fast Drinker	211
20 and Over	212

Vodka Cocktails

Green Island

Ingredients:
30 ml. Apple Vodka
30 ml. Regular Vodka
10 ml. Sweet & Sour
50 ml. Apple Juice

Directions:
Put all of the ingredients in a shaker, along with a few ice cubes. Shake and place it in a long glass. Garnish with apple, lemons and other seasonal fruit.

Last Rainbow

Ingredients:
15 ml. Grenadine
15 ml. Cherry Liqueur – Red
20 ml. Orange Juice
20 ml. Pineapple Juice
5 ml. Grenadine – Orange
20 ml. Apple Vodka
30 ml. Midori - Green
30 ml. Vodka
15 ml. Blue Curacao- Blue

Directions:
This cocktail is done in a few steps. It must be carefully done so the colors don't get mixed. For the first color (Red) put grenadine and cherry liqueur in the shaker and then place it in a long glass. Put crushed ice. The second layer is (Orange), so mix Grenadine, Orange Juice and Pineapple Juice. Place crushed ice. For the third layer (Green), put Midori and Apple Vodka and put it on top of the ice. Finally, add Vodka and Blue Curacao and put everything on top.

Maraboo

Ingredients:

Yellow layer:
10 ml. Vodka
30 ml. Pineapple Juice
30 ml Orange Juice
10 ml. Green Lime Juice

Blue Layer:
15 ml. Coconut Vodka or Malibu
15 ml. Banana Rum
15 ml. Blue Curacao
40 ml. Sprite

Directions:

For the yellow layer, use the first three ingredients. Place it in a shaker and pour it in a small glass. Put crushed ice and then the rest of the alcohol put it in the shaker, so at the end it has a blue color. Garnish the glass with coconut sugar (preferably white) and a cherry.

Sweet Chocolate

Ingredients:
30 ml. Vodka
10 ml. Chocolate Vodka
30 ml. Caramel Syrup
Half Banana
45 ml. Milk

Directions:
Put the Vodka and the Caramel syrup in a shaker and shake it. Pour these liquids in a glass, and then blend half banana with milk and some ice. Place it in the glass. Garnish with whipped cream, cocoa and banana peel.

Umbrella

Ingredients:
30 ml. Vodka
10 ml. Lime Juice
20 ml. Malibu
15. ml Blue Curacao
15 ml. Grenadine
40 ml. Raspberry Soda

Directions:
Put the Grenadine first. Put the rest of the ingredients in a shaker. Place a few green limes in the glass and then pour the alcohol from the shaker. Garnish with green or blue sugar and an umbrella.

Blue Sky

Ingredients:
30 ml. Vodka
30 ml. Raspberry Vodka
30 ml. Peach Schnapps
15 ml. Peach Juice
10 ml. Sweet & Sour
10 ml. Blue Curacao

Directions:
Put all of the ingredients in the shaker, except for the Blue Curacao. Shake it and put it in a small glass. Add the Blue Curacao on top and garnish it with a few blueberries.

Lady in Pink

Ingredients:
60 ml. Vodka
30 ml Cointreau
30 ml. Triple Sec
40 ml. Sweet & Sour
20. Pink Kinky

Directions:
Put all of the ingredients except for the Pink Kinky in a shaker. Shake it and put it in a small glass. Add the Pink kinky on top and garnish with a few strawberries.

Kiss on the Lips

Ingredients:
40 ml. Vodka
15ml. Baileys
10 ml. Sweet & Sour
60 ml. Pineapple Juice

Directions:
Put all of the ingredients in a shaker and after that pour them in a long glass. Garnish the glass with white sugar and put fruit on the top of the glass.

Vodkaland

Ingredients
30 ml. Mango Vodka
10 ml. Vodka
20 ml. Sweet & Sour
40 ml. Mango Juice

Directions:
Put all of the ingredients in a shaker along with a few ice cubes. Garnish the glass with mango and put some inside the glass too.

Watermelon Kiss

Ingredients:
30 ml. Vodka
20 ml. Watermelon Pucker
20 ml. Triple Sec
A few tablespoons of real Watermelon

Directions:
Place the few tablespoons of watermelon in the glass. Shake the alcohol and pour it into the glass. Mix the ingredients with a spoon. Garnish with a small watermelon slice.

Zombie

Ingredients:
30 ml. Vodka
20 ml. Bacardi
60 ml. Pineapple Juice
20 ml. Orange Juice
20 ml. Midori

Directions:
Put all of the ingredients in a shaker and place them in a Martini glass. Garnish it with some green apple or other green fruit.

The Last Sunset

Ingredients:
30 ml. Vodka
10 ml. Tequila
5 ml. Triple Sec
20 ml. Malibu
30 ml. Orange Juice
30 ml. Pineapple Juice
15 ml. Grenadine

Directions:
Put Grenadine in a Martini glass. Add the rest of the ingredients in a shaker with some ice cubes. Put everything in a glass and garnish with a pineapple and an umbrella.

The Alligator

Ingredients:
30 ml. Vodka
20 ml. Menthol Crème
10 ml. Sambuca

Directions:
Put all of the ingredients in a shaker and garnish with some green leaves.

Sea Waters

Ingredients:
30 ml. Vodka
30 ml. Sweet & Sour
10 ml. Triple Sec
40 ml. Sprite or Sparkling Water
10 ml. Triple Sec

Directions:
Put all of the ingredients in a shaker, except for the Sparkling water or the Sprite. Pour it in a glass and add the water on top. Mix it with a tablespoon and garnish it with lemon and green apple.

Vodka Schnapps

Ingredients:
30 ml. Vodka
20 ml. Archers
40 ml. Sparkling Water
10 ml. Triple Sec

Directions:
Put the Vodka, Triple Sec and Archers in the shaker. Shake it and pour it in a wine glass. Add the sparkling water on top. Place orange peel in the glass.

Madrid

Ingredients:
30 ml. Vodka
40 ml. Cranberry Juice
20 ml. Orange Juice
10 ml. Lemonade
10 ml. Grenadine

Directions:
Shake all of the ingredients and pour it in a small glass. Add a few lemons and limes in the glass.

Purple Poison

Ingredients:
30 ml. Vodka
15 ml. Blue Curacao
30 ml. Cranberry Juice
30 ml. Pineapple Juice
10 ml. Sweet & Sour
15 ml. Grenadine

Directions:
Shake all of the ingredients together until you get a dark purple color. Pour it in a long glass and garnish it with some mint leaves.

Coconut Island

Ingredients:
30 ml. Vodka
15 ml. Archers
10 ml. Malibu
20 ml. Orange Juice
20 ml. Cranberry Juice

Directions:
Put all of the ingredients in a shaker. Serve the drink in a long glass garnished with a slice of pineapple and coconut.

Monkey's Booze

Ingredients:
30 ml. Vodka
20 ml. Banana Vodka
10 ml. Baileys
30 ml. Pineapple Juice

Directions:
Place all of the ingredients in a shaker and then pour it in a long glass. Garnish it with some banana peel and menthol leaves.

La Mariposa

Ingredients:
35 ml. Vodka
40 ml. Grapefruit Juice
10 ml. Green Lemon Juice
10 ml. Cointreau
15 ml. Grenadine

Directions:
Put the Vodka and Juices in a shaker with a few ice cubes. Put it in a medium glass and add the Grenadine on top. Add some pineapple leaves inside and a cherry.

Rum Cocktails

Antman

Ingredients:
30 ml. Dark Rum
10 ml. Bacardi
40 ml. Orange Juice
1 spoon of brown sugar

Directions:
Mix all of the ingredients in a shaker with a few ice cubes. Put it all in a long glass and garnish it with brown sugar and orange peel.

La Passion

Ingredients:
30ml. Bacardi
10ml. Lemon Juice
25 ml. Triple Sec
25ml. Blue Curacao

Directions:
Put all of the ingredients in a shaker and shake it good. Serve the drink in a martini glass and garnish it with green lime.

Captain Jack

Ingredients:
40 ml. Dark Rum
20 ml. Coconut Rum
10 ml. Coconut Juice
25 ml. Orange Juice
25 ml. Pineapple Juice

Directions:
Mix all of the ingredients in a shaker with a few ice cubes. Put everything in a medium glass with few oranges in it. Garnish with two black straws and a small pineapple.

Lucy

Ingredients:
30 ml. Bacardi
40 ml. Tangerine Juice
2 spoons of dark sugar
20 ml. Grenadine

Directions:
Take 3-4 tangerines and squeeze them, until you have juice. Put it in a shaker then add the sugar and the rum. Put it in a glass and then add the Grenadine. Garnish the glass with tangerine peel and rosemary.

Sunshine

Ingredients:
30 ml. Dark Rum
25 ml. Orange Juice
25 ml. Pineapple Juice
10 ml. Green Lime Juice
10 ml. Gin
25 ml. Grenadine

Directions:
Put the alcohol (except for the gin and grenadine) in a shaker. Shake it good and then add the rest of the ingredients on top. Mix it with a spoon and put some green lime and orange in the glass. Serve it in a normal glass and garnish it with some pineapple on top.

Dark Captain

Ingredients:
30 ml. Dark Rum
10 ml. Vodka
5 ml. Bacardi
40ml. Lemon Juice

Directions:
Mix all of the ingredients in a shaker filled with ice and pour it in a long glass. Garnish it with a few lemon circles and rosemary.

Magician

Ingredients:
20 ml. Coconut Rum
30 ml. Dark Rum
25 ml. Jagermeister
40 ml. Orange Juice

Directions:
Put all of the ingredients in a shaker filled with ice cubes and shake. Put everything in a long glass and garnish with brown sugar and a few orange circles.

Mango Mania

Ingredients:
30 ml. Dark Rum
10 ml. Green lime juice
50 ml. Mango Juice
Half blended Mango

Directions:
Blend the mango first and put it in a glass. Add the dark rum, green lime juice and mango juice in the shaker and put some ice. Mix these ingredients well and then add it in the glass. With a tablespoon mix all well again, and garnish the glass with few mango slices.

Monday

Ingredients:
30 ml. Dark Rum
20 ml. Malibu
10 ml. Banana Liqueur
30 ml. Orange Juice
20 ml. Grenadine

Directions:
Mix all ingredients well, and then put it in a glass along with some orange slices. Garnish with banana peel and a few oranges.

Gambit

Ingredients:
25 ml. Bacardi
15 ml. Malibu
10 ml. Amaretto
30 ml. Orange Juice
30 ml. Pineapple Juice

Directions:
Mix all ingredients together, and serve it in a medium glass. Garnish with brown sugar and pineapple slice.

Summer days

Ingredients:
30 ml. Bacardi
10 ml. Tequila
20 ml. Blue Curacao
20 ml. Melon liqueur

Directions:
Mix all ingredients in a shaker with a few ice cubes. Shake until you get a nice green color. Add it in a hurricane glass and garnish it with melon slice and a cherry.

Bitter Love

Ingredients:
30 ml. Dark Rum
5 ml. Angostura Bitters
5 ml. Green Lime Juice
1 spoon of sugar
40 ml. Sprite

Directions:
Mix all of the ingredients together in a glass and garnish it with some lime circle.

Fast & Furious

Ingredients:
30 ml. Dark Rum
20 ml. Orange Liqueur
20 ml. Triple Sec
10 ml. Fresh Lime Juice
20. Raspberry Juice

Directions:
Put all of the ingredients in a shaker and mix it well. Add everything in a martini glass, and garnish it with some orange peel and rosemary.

Zeus

Ingredients:
30 ml. Bacardi
10 ml. Vermouth
15 ml. Triple Sec
40 ml. Sprite

Directions:
Combine all of the ingredients and put them in a shaker with a few ice cubes. Shake it and serve the cocktail in a medium glass, garnished with green lime and menthol leaves.

Empty Island

Ingredients
30 ml. Bacardi
10 ml Triple Sec
40 ml. Strawberry Juice
10 ml. Grenadine

Directions:
Combine all of the ingredients and shake them well. Add the liquids in a long glass and garnish it with a strawberry and menthol leaves.

Cool Kid

30 ml. Bacardi
10 ml. Dark Rum
10 ml. Malibu
40 ml. Coconut Milk
30 ml. Orange Juice
30 ml. Pineapple Juice

Directions:
Mix all of the ingredients together until you have a beautiful white mixture. Decorate the glass with a cinnamon stick, cocoa and strawberry or cherry.

Coke Rum

Ingredients:
30ml. Bacardi
70ml. Coca Cola
20ml. Green Lime Juice

Directions:
Put Bacardi and Green Lime juice in a shaker and mix it all. Add this in a long glass and pour Coca Cola on top. Garnish the glass with green lime and mint leaves.

Green Poison

Ingredients
30 ml. Bacardi
10 ml. Apple Vodka
20 ml. Midori
40 ml. Apple Juice

Directions:
Mix all of the ingredients in a shaker with a few ice cubes. Pour the liquids in a martini glass and garnish it with rosemary and apple slice.

LianYu

Ingredients:
35 ml. DarkRum
45 ml. Mango Soda
20 ml. Grenadine

Directions:
Put the dark rum in a glass and add the soda. There is no need to shake anything, so mixing with tablespoon will be enough. When you finish with these two ingredients, add the grenadine on top. Garnish with some mango slices and a cherry.

Banana Rum

30 ml. Banana Rum
20 ml. Coconut Rum
40 ml. Pineapple Juice
20 ml. Grenadine

Directions:
Mix all of the ingredients in a shaker filled with ice. Pour the liquids in a long glass and garnish it with a banana peel.

GIN Cocktails

The Beast

30 ml. Gin
10 ml. Sweet & Sour
35 ml. Lemonade
40 ml. Tonic water

Directions:
Mix the gin, sweet & sour and lemonade together in a shaker with some ice cubes. Pour it in a glass and then add the tonic water. Garnish with some lemons and kiwi.

Genius

30 ml. Gin
10 ml. Archers
45 ml. Peach Ice Tea
10 ml. Triple Sec

Directions:
Mix all of the ingredients in a shaker with some ice cubes and pour it in a long glass with crushed ice. Put lemons and peach in the glass and add archers. Garnish the glass with oranges and mint leaves.

Black Canary

40 ml. Gin
25 ml. Blueberry Syrup
10 ml. Vodka
40 ml. Sparkling Water

Directions:
Mix the gin, blueberry syrup and vodka together in a shaker with ice. Put it in a medium glass and add the sparkling water on top. Garnish the glass with some blueberries and peach.

The Man

30 ml. Gin
40 ml. Apple Juice (clear)
20 ml. Strawberry syrup
40 ml. Sprite

Directions:
Mix the gin, apple juice and strawberry syrup in a shaker. Fill a long glass with crushed ice and pour the alcohol. Add the sprite on top and garnish the glass with green apples.

Samba

Ingredients:
30 ml. Gin
20 ml. Peach Syrup
10 ml. Sweet & Sour
20 ml. Fanta

Directions:
Put the gin, peach syrup and sweet and sour in a shaker with ice cubes. Add the ingredients in a martini glass and pour Fanta on top. Garnish the glass with peach and lemons.

The Big Bang

Ingredients:
30 ml. Gin
30 ml. Cherry juice
20 ml. Lemonade
10 ml. Green Apple Vodka

Directions:
Add all of the ingredients in a shaker and mix them well with some ice cubes. Pour everything in a martini glass and garnish with some cherries on a stick.

Lost

Ingredients:
30 ml. Gin
20 ml. Dark Rum
40 ml. Pineapple Juice
20 ml. Grenadine

Directions:
Put gin, dark rum and pineapple juice in a shaker with a few ice cubes. Add the ingredients in a medium glass and pour the grenadine. Garnish the glass with pineapple slices.

Tropico

Ingredients:
30 ml. Gin
20 ml. Grapefruit Vodka
20 ml. Melon liqueur
40 ml. 7 up

Directions:
Put gin, grapefruit vodka and melon liqueur in a shaker with a few ice cubes. Shake it and pour it in martini glass and add 7 up on top. Garnish the glass with green lime.

The Secret Alley

Ingredients:
30 ml. Gin
20 ml. Banana Liquor
30 ml. Tropical Mix Juice

Directions:
Put all of the ingredients in a shaker with a few ice cubes. Shake it well and pour it in a medium glass filled with fruit. Garnish the glass with rosemary.

The Bear

Ingredients:
30 ml. Gin
20 ml. Pear Juice or syrup
30 ml. Sweet & Sour

Directions:
Mix all of the ingredients in a shaker and pour them in a glass with crushed ice. Garnish the glass with some pears.

Duty Free

Ingredients:
30 ml. Gin
20 ml. Lemonade
10 ml. Watermelon liqueur
+ Watermelon

Directions:
Scoop some watermelon and put it in a glass. Add the gin, lemonade and watermelon liqueur in a shaker filled with ice. Shake it and add the liquids in the glass. Garnish it with some watermelon slices.

Lost Pirate

Ingredients
30 ml. Gin
30 ml. Bacardi
20 ml. Dark Rum
50 ml. Sparkling Water

Directions:
Mix all of the ingredients except for the sparkling water. Put them in a glass filled with peach slices and add the sparkling water on top.

Friday the 13th

Ingredients:
30 ml. Gin
20 ml. Triple Sec
30 ml. Green Lime Juice
50 ml. Schweppes

Directions:
Put the gin, triple sec and lime juice in a shaker filled with ice. Add the Schweppes on top and garnish the glass with red lime and mint leaves.

Dark Summer Night

Ingredients:
30 ml. Gin
30 ml. Malibu
30 ml. Blue Curacao
45 ml. 7 up

Directions:
Add gin, malibu and blue curacao in a shaker with a few ice cubes. Add 7 up on the top and garnish the glass with a few blueberries.

Forestberry

Ingredients:
30 ml. Gin
40 ml. Cranberry Juice
20 ml. Triple Sec
10 ml. Grenadine

Directions:
Mix gin, triple sec and cranberry juice in a shaker filled with ice. Pour the grenadine on top and garnish the glass with strawberries or blueberries.

Camping Gin

Ingredients:
30 ml. Gin
30 ml. Vermouth
40 ml. Campari
60 ml. Orange Juice

Directions:
Mix all of the ingredients in a shaker with a few ice cubes and add them in a wine glass. Put oranges in the glass.

Gringo

Ingredients:
30 ml. Gin
30 ml. Menthol liqueuer
40 ml. Sprite

Directions:
Put gin and menthol liqueur in a shaker with some ice cubes. Mix it well and add sprite on top. Serve this drink in a martini glass with menthol leafs.

Creamy Gin

Ingredients:
30 ml. Gin
30 ml. Lemonade
20 ml. Lemon Juice (fresh)
1 tablespoon of sugar
20 ml. Cream

Directions:
Mix all of the ingredients in a shaker along with a few ice cubes and put it in a long glass. Garnish the glass with a few lemons and menthol leaf.

Apricot Love Potion

Ingredients:
30 ml. Gin
40 ml. Apricot liqueur
20 ml. Grenadine

Directions:
Mix all of the ingredients in a shaker along with a few ice cubes and put it in a medium glass and garnish the glass with a few apple slices.

Sugar Mama

Ingredients:
30 ml. Gin
20 ml. Lavander Syrup
40 ml. 7 up
20 ml. Lime Juice

Directions:
Put all of the ingredients (except for the 7up) and mix them well. Put them in a glass with some strawberries and blueberries and then add 7 up. Garnish the glass with lavender.

Tequila Cocktails

Mariachi

Ingredients:
30 ml. Tequila Gold
20 ml. Tequila Silver
35 ml. Pineapple Juice
35 ml. Orange Juice
25 ml. Orange Liqueur

Directions:
Mix all of the ingredients in a shaker full with ice cubes. Serve this cocktail in a long glass and garnish it with some orange slices and mint leaves.

Industrial

Ingredients:
30 ml. Tequila
20 ml. Gin
20 ml. Vodka
35 ml Melon Liqueur

Directions:
Mix all of the ingredients together in a shaker full with ice. Pour the liquids in a long glass and garnish the glass with melon slice.

Dragonfly

Ingredients:
40 ml. Tequila
20 ml. Jagermeister
20 ml. Orange Liqueur
40 ml. Orange Juice

Directions:
Mix all of the ingredients together in a shaker full with ice. Pour the liquids in a long glass and garnish it with some orange slices.

Texas Rangers

Ingredients:
30 ml. Tequila
20 ml. Cointreau
30 ml. Triple Sec
60 ml. Pineapple Juice

Directions:
Mix all of the ingredients together in a shaker with crushed ice. Pour everything in a medium glass garnished with pineapple slice and leaves.

Insideus

Ingredients:
30 ml. Tequila
20 ml. Amaretto
35 ml. Lemonade
40 ml. Coca Cola
1 tablespoon sugar

Directions:
Mix all of the ingredients together with a tablespoon. Fill the glass with a lot of ice and lemons, and garnish it with some mint leaves.

Sexy Margarita

Ingredients:
30 ml. White Tequila
40 ml. Watermelon Liqueur
20 ml. Sparkling Water

Directions:
Add all of the ingredients in a margarita glass and garnish it with sugar and some watermelon slice.

Peachy Tequila

Ingredients:
30 ml. Tequila
20 ml. Peach Syrup
30 ml. Archer

Directions:
Mix all of the ingredients together in a glass filled with ice. Garnish the glass with peach slices.

Uptown

Ingredients:
30 ml. Gold Tequila
20 ml. Sweet & Sour Mix
10 ml. Orange Syrup
30 ml. Sparkling Water

Directions:
Mix all of the ingredients together in a shaker, except for the sparkling water, which you should add it on top. Put some orange slices in the glass and garnish it with some seasonal fruit.

La Manche

Ingredients:
30 ml. Tequila
20 ml. Schweppes
15 ml. Sweet & Sour

Directions:
Mix all of the ingredients in a glass and stir it with a tablespoon. Garnish the glass with a few lemon slices.

Apple Tequila

Ingredients:
30 ml. Tequila
20 ml. Apple Syrup
20 ml. Apple Juice
10 ml. Midori

Directions:
Mix all of the ingredients together in a shaker filled with ice. Pour it in big martini glass and garnish it with sugar and green apple slice.

Lost Captain Jack

Ingredients:
30 ml. Tequila
30 ml. Orange Soda
20 ml. Dark Rum
20 ml. Grenadine

Directions:
Mix all of the ingredients together in a shaker filled with ice. Pour it in a long glass and garnish the glass with orange slices.

Rimini

Ingredients:
30 ml. Tequila
20 ml. Bacardi
20 ml. Jagermeister
40 ml. Tonic Water

Directions:
Mix all of the ingredients (except for the Tonic Water) which should be on top. Stir with a tablespoon and garnish the glass with a few lemons and oranges.

Don Agosto

Ingredients:
30 ml. Tequila
40 ml. Agave Nectar
20 ml. Fresh Lime Juice
20 ml. Lemonade

Directions:
Mix all of the ingredients together in a shaker filled with lot of ice, and then add some crushed ice in a long glass. Garnish the glass with lemons and some mint leaves.

The more the better

Ingredients:
30 ml. Tequila
20 ml. Cherry Syrup
20 ml. Grenadine
60 ml. Sparkling Water

Directions:
Mix all of the ingredients together in a shaker (except for the sparkling water) which should be added on top. Put everything in a big martini glass and garnish it with white sugar and a cherry.

Margarita Island

Ingredients:
30 ml. Tequila
20 ml. Malibu
40 ml. Coconut Milk
20 ml. Amaretto

Directions:
Mix all of the ingredients together in a shaker and fill a medium glass with all these ingredients. Garnish the glass with coconut sugar and some cocoa.

Mexican Waters

Ingredients:
30 ml. White Tequila
20 ml. Triple Sec
20 ml. Vanilla Syrup
50 ml. Pineapple Juice

Directions:
Mix all of the ingredients together in a shaker filled with ice. Garnish the glass with a pineapple slice.

Mayan Secret

Ingredients:
30 ml. White Tequila
20 ml. Campari
20 ml. Orange Syrup
20 ml. Champagne

Directions:
Put all of the ingredients together in a margarita glass and stir with a tablespoon. Garnish the glass with a small orange slice.

Cancun Moonlight

Ingredients:
30 ml. Silver Tequila
20 ml. Cointreau
10 ml. Cognac
40 ml. Mango Nectar
20 ml. Orange Syrup
15 ml. Grenadine

Directions:
Mix all of the ingredients together in a shaker filled with ice. Pour everything in a medium glass and garnish it with an orange peel.

Cocktail Del Carmen

Ingredients:
30 ml. Silver Tequila
30 ml. Sweet & Sour
35 ml. Lemonade
25 ml. Blue Curacao

Directions:
Mix all of the ingredients together (except for the blue curacao) in a shaker filled with ice. Pour everything in a medium glass and then add the blue curacao.

Night in Acapulco

Ingredients:
30 ml. White Tequila
20 ml. Blueberry Syrup
30 ml. Blueberry Juice
20 ml. Bacardi

Directions:
Mix all of the ingredients together in a shaker full with ice. Garnish the glass with some blueberries.

Liqueur Cocktails

Spring Vacation

Ingredients:
10ml Kiwi syrup
45ml gin
10ml lemon juice
25 ml. Vodka

Directions:
Pour all ingredients into a shaker with ice cubes. Pour the liquids in a cocktails glass and garnish it with a slice of kiwi.

Perl of Harbor

Ingredients:
15ml Baileys
40ml Vodka
30ml. Strawberry Liqueur
45 ml. Jagermeister

Directions:
Mix all of the ingredients along with a few ice cubes and place them in a martini glass. Garnish the glass with a strawberry.

Maroon 5

Ingredients:
40 ml. Watermelon liqueur
20 ml. Strawberry liqueur
25 ml. Vodka
10 ml. Blue Curacao

Directions:
Mix the liqueurs in a shaker with ice cubes and place them in a long glass. Put crushed ice and add blue curacao on top.

Cocktail Pie

Ingredients:
30 ml. Apple liqueur
10 ml. Vodka
20 ml. Tequila
5 ml. Triple Sec
60 ml. Apple Juice

Directions:
Mix all of the ingredients well and put the cocktail in a martini glass. Garnish it with apple slice and rosemary.

Banana Daiquiri

Ingredients:
40 ml. Banana Liqueur
10 ml. Tequila
30 ml. Dark Rum

Directions:
All the ingredients in a shaker full with ice and mix it well. Make sure that you put a lot of ice in the glass, and then add the already prepared ingredients. Garnish the glass with banana peel.

Kiwi cream martini

Ingredients:
30 ml. Kiwi Liqueur
30 ml. Sprite
20 ml. Vodka
40 ml. Midori

Directions:
Mix all of the ingredients except for the Sprite. Put it in a long glass with crushed ice and add the alcohol. Then put the sprite on top and garnish the glass with kiwi.

Frozen Yogurt

Ingredients:
45 ml. Strawberry liqueur
20 ml. Sweet & Sour
20 ml. Cake Vodka
1 yogurt

Directions:
Put the strawberry liqueur and yogurt in a blender with a lot of ice. When it is done, place them in the shaker and add vodka and sweet & sour. When all if well mixed, you can put it in a glass and garnish it with a strawberry.

Cold Pear

Ingredients:
30 ml. Pear Liqueur
20 ml. Archers
10 ml. Pear Juice
40 ml. Sparkling Water

Directions:
Put pear liqueur, pear juice and archers and mix them in a shaker along with a few ice cubes. Add the sparkling water on top and garnish the glass with some pear slice or just add the cocktail in a martini glass and put rosemary on top.

SnowWhite

Ingredients:
30 ml. Pear Liqueur
20 ml. Milk
25 ml. Lemonade
40 ml. 7UP

Directions:
Put Pear liqueur, milk and lemonade in a shaker and mix it well. Add 7 up on top and garnish the glass with some fruit.

Mango Spiced

Ingredients:
30 ml. Mango liqueur
60 ml. Orange Juice
25 ml. Grenadine
35 ml. Pineapple Juice

Directions:
Mix all of the ingredients together and add them in a long glass. Garnish the glass with some oranges.

Speedy Gonzales

Ingredients:
30 ml. Menthe liqueur
30 ml. Vodka
20 ml. Bacardi
40 ml. Water
1 tablespoon green food coloring

Directions:
Mix all of the ingredients together with a lot of ice. Put them in a martini glass and garnish it with a cherry.

Poirot

Ingredients:
30 ml. Blue Curacao Liqueur
30 ml. Banana Liqueur
30 ml. Coconut Rum
30 ml. Bacardi

Directions:
Mix all of the ingredients and add them in a Martini glass. Garnish the glass with orange peel.

Incandescent

Ingredients:
30 ml. Khalua coffee liqueur
20ml. Bailey's
10 ml. Archers
40 ml. Pineapple Juice

Directions:
Mix all of the ingredients together and put them in a medium glass. Garnish the glass with a pineapple slice.

Shadowspire

Ingredients:
30 ml. Safari liqueur
20 ml. Blue Curacao Liqueur
20 ml. Orange Juice
20 ml. Pineapple Juice

Directions:
Put the safari liqueur along with the juices and mix them well in a shaker filled with ice. Put everything in a glass and then add the blue curacao. Garnish the glass with orange and pineapple on a stick.

Summer in Greece

Ingredients:
30 ml. Hpnotiq liqueur
20 ml. Midori
35 ml. Lemonade
40 ml. Sparkling Water

Directions:
Put hpnotiq, midori and lemonade in a shaker and mix them with a lot of ice. Serve in a medium glass and then add the sparkling water.

Sidari Sunshine

Ingredients:
30 ml. Khalua coffee liqueur
20 ml. Dark Rum
20 ml. Orange Juice
20 ml. Milk Cream
20 ml. Orange Liqueur

Directions:
Put khalua, dark rum and orange juice and mix them with ice. Put them in a circle glass and prepare the cream. Put Milk cream in a shaker with the orange liqueur and mix it well. Add it on the top and garnish the glass with oranges and cocoa.

Hide and Seek

Ingredients:
30 ml. Khalua coffee liqueur
10 ml. Amaretto
30 ml. Vodka
10 ml. Bacardi
Whipped Cream

Directions:
Put khalua, amaretto, vodka and Bacardi in a shaker and mix it well. Pour it in a long glass and garnish it with some whipped cream and coffee.

Hypnotiser

Ingredients:
30 ml. Strawberry Liqueur
35 ml. Vodka
20 ml. Gin
80 ml. Lemon & lime soda
20 ml. Sweet & Sour

Directions:
Mix all ingredients together and serve this drink in a medium glass. Put some menthe and strawberries in the glass and garnish it with green lime.

Fiji

Ingredients:
20 ml. Pear liqueur
45 ml. Dark Rum
80 ml. Pineapple Juice
20 ml. Lime Juice

Directions:
Mix all of the ingredients together and put them in a medium glass filled with ice. Put some pineapples inside.

Adventures

Ingredients:
30 ml. Mango Liqueur
40 ml. Bacardi
80 ml. Watermelon Juice
40 ml. Coconut Milk

Directions:
Mix all of the ingredients together until you have a beautiful pink color. Garnish the glass with slice of watermelon.

Whiskey Cocktails

The Real Godfather

Ingredients:
30 ml. Whiskey (Jameson)
20 ml. Vermouth
30 ml. Coca Cola

Directions:
Put all of the ingredients in a short glass and garnish with a cherry.

Don Juan

Ingredients:
30 ml. Whiskey (Jim Beam)
20 ml. Lavander Syrup
30 ml. Sparkling Water

Directions:
Put everything in a martini glass and stir with a tablespoon. Garnish the glass with rosemary.

New York's Mystery Lady

Ingredients:
30 ml. Whiskey (Jack Daniels)
20 ml. Amaretto
10 ml. Khalua
Whipped Cream

Directions:
Put the Whiskey, amaretto and khalua in a shaker filled with crushed ice. Mix it well and add it in a long glass. Garnish the glass with whipped cream and some sparkles.

Jack's Special

Ingredients:
40 ml Whiskey (Jack Daniels)
20 ml. Sweet & Sour
40 ml. Lemon-lime soda

Directions:
Put all of the ingredients in a glass along with a few ice cubes. Mix it well with a tablespoon and garnish the glass with some lemon or lime circles.

LadyBug

Ingredients:
30 ml. Whiskey (Jameson)
40 ml. Blood Orange Juice
20 ml. Orange Syrup
10 ml. Triple Sec
10 ml. Cherry Liqueur

Directions:
Mix everything in a shaker filled with ice cubes and serve the drink in a short glass with an orange.

Watermelon Whiskey

Ingredients:
30 ml. Whiskey
20 ml. Watermelon Syrup
10 ml. Smirnoff Chocolate Vodka
20 ml. Sparkling water

Directions:
Put all of the ingredients in a shaker filled with ice. Mix everything well and then pour it in a long glass. Garnish the glass with watermelon slice.

Frozen Whiskey Time

Ingredients:
30 ml. Whiskey (Jameson or Jack Daniels)
3 scoops Vanilla Yogurt
30 ml. Strawberry Syrup
30 ml. Raspberry Syrup

Directions:
Put raspberry syrup, strawberry syrup and vanilla yogurt in a blender and mix everything well. Add the whiskey in a long glass and then put the cream on top. Garnish the glass with some fruit.

Summer Whiskey

Ingredients:
30 ml. Whiskey
40 ml. Somersby Blueberry Cider
20 ml. Blueberry Syrup (Monin)

Directions:
Put whiskey and blueberry syrup in a shaker filled with ice. Mix it well and then pour it in a medium glass. Add Somersby on top and stir it with a tablespoon. Garnish the glass with blueberries and menthol leaves.

Whiskey Lemonade

Ingredients:
30 ml. Whiskey (Jim Beam)
30 ml. Lemonade
10 ml. Mango Juice

Directions:
Mix all of the ingredients together in a shaker filled with ice. Add everything in a big martini glass and garnish it with white sugar, lemon and menthol leaves.

Apple Bourbon

Ingredients:
30 ml. Whiskey (Jim Beam)
20 ml. Apple Syrup
30 ml. Apple Juice
20 ml. Somersby Apple Cider

Directions:
Put whiskey, apple syrup and apple juice in a shaker with crushed ice. Mix it all well and add it in a long glass. Put Somersby on top, and mix it with a tablespoon.
Garnish the glass with some apple slices.

Amaretto Whiskey

Ingredients:
30 ml. Whiskey (Johnnie Walker Red)
20 ml. Amaretto
10 ml. Khalua
50 ml. Coca Cola

Directions:
Put whiskey, amaretto and khalua in a shaker filled with ice. Shake it well and then pour it in a short glass. Add coca cola on top and mix it well with a tablespoon. Garnish the glass with a cherry.

Whiskey Sleeping Pill

Ingredients:
35 ml. Whiskey (Johnnie Walker Black)
10 ml. Malibu rum
10 ml. Pineapple Juice
20 ml. Cranberry Juice

Directions:
Mix all of the ingredients in a shaker filled with ice cubes. Pour the liquids in a medium glass and garnish it with a few orange slices.

Mint Whiskey

Ingredients:
30 ml. Whiskey (Jameson)
20 ml. Menthol Liqueur
40 ml. Coca Cola

Directions:
Mix the whiskey and menthol liqueur together in a shaker filled with ice. Then, add the coca cola and mix with a tablespoon. Garnish the glass with lemon and menthol leaves.

Rainstorm

Ingredients:
30 ml. Whiskey
20 ml. Gin
30 ml. Peach Liqueur
40 ml. Sparkling Water

Directions:
Mix whiskey, peach liqueur and gin together in a shaker filled with ice. Pour the liquids in a medium glass and add the sparkling water. Garnish the glass with seasonal fruit.

Sweet Gentleman

Ingredients:
30ml. Whiskey
20 ml. Midori Liqueur
25 ml. Baileys

Directions:
Mix all of the ingredients together in a shaker filled with ice. Serve the drink in a short glass and garnish it with some seasonal fruit.

Brown Whiskey

Ingredients:
30 ml. Whiskey (Jack Daniels)
20 ml. Macadamia Nut Syrup (Monin)
40 ml. Coca Cola

Directions:
Mix all of the ingredients together and serve the drink in a medium glass. Garnish it with some seasonal fruit.

Sweet Fruity Whiskey

Ingredients:
30 ml. Whiskey
20 ml. Blood Orange Syrup
10 ml. Blackberry Syrup
40 ml. Orange Juice

Directions:
Mix all of the ingredients in a shaker filled with ice. Pour the ingredients in a long glass and garnish it with some orange and apple slices.

Banana Whiskey

Ingredients:

35 ml. Whiskey
20 ml. Banana Syrup
40 ml. 7 Up

Directions:
Put all of the ingredients in a glass and mix it well with a tablespoon. Garnish the glass with banana peel.

Caramel Whiskey

Ingredients:
30 ml. Whiskey
20 ml. Caramel Syrup
40 ml. Coca Cola

Directions:
Put all of the ingredients together in a glass and mix it well with a tablespoon. Garnish the glass with some brown sugar.

Spring Breeze

Ingredients:
30 ml. Whiskey (Jameson)
20 ml. Chocolate Mint Syrup
40 ml. Coca cola

Directions:
Put all of the ingredients together in a small glass and mix it well with a tablespoon. Garnish the glass with some menthol leaves.

WINE COCKTAILS

Red Russian

Ingredients:
30 ml. White Wine
35 ml. Campari
40 ml. Orange Juice
10ml. Sparkling Water

Directions:
Put the white wine, Campari and orange juice in a shaker and mix them well along with some ice cubes. Serve the liquids in a big wine glass, and add the sparkling water on top. Garnish the glass with slices of orange and a cherry.

Big Foot

Ingredients:
30 ml. Pineapple Moscato Wine
20 ml. Cranberry Juice
20 ml. Archers
10 ml. Sprite

Directions:
Put everything in a big glass and mix it well with a tablespoon. Garnish the glass with pineapple and some leaves.

Santorini Paradise

Ingredients:
30 ml. White Wine
40 ml. Sprite
25 ml. Triple Sec
20 ml. Green Lime Juice
25 ml. Blue Curacao

Directions:
Put the wine along with the juices and triple sec in a glass, and then add the blue curacao on top. Garnish the glass with green lime peel.

Moscato

Ingredients:
40 ml. Strawberry Moscato Wine
25 ml. Strawberry Juice
20 ml. Watermelon liqueur
20 ml. Grenadine

Directions:
Put the wine, strawberry juice and watermelon liqueur in a glass, along with some ice cubes and then add the grenadine on top.
Garnish the glass with a strawberry.

White Magic

Ingredients:
45 ml. White Wine
30 ml. Brandy
100 ml. Sparkling Water
1 tablespoon of honey

Directions:
Put the white wine in the glass. Add the brandy and the honey the glass, and pour the sparkling water on top. Garnish the glass with a few lemons and orange.

Drunk

Ingredients:
30 ml. White Wine
20 ml. Strawberry Vodka
30 ml. Strawberry Syrup
40 ml. Sparkling water

Directions:
Put the strawberry syrup and Vodka in the glass. Then add the wine and the sparkling water on top, and mix them with a tablespoon. Garnish the glass with a lot of strawberries and some menthol leaves.

F.R.I.E.N.D.S

Ingredients:
30 ml. Rose Wine
45 ml. Seagrams Escapes (Wild Berries)
+ Strawberries and Blueberries

Directions:
Put the strawberries and blueberries in the glass and then add the wine and Seagrams Escapes. Let the fruit soak the liquids and then mix it with a tablespoon. Garnish the glass with a strawberry and rosemary.

Blueberry Sauvignon

Ingredients:
45 ml. Sauvignon Blanc
35 ml. Lemonade
40 ml. Blueberry Juice
+ mint leaves

Directions:
Put the mint leaves in the glass then add the lemonade, blueberry juice and the wine on top. Mix them with a tablespoon and garnish the glass with a few blueberries and mint leaves.

Bloody Wine

Ingredients:
30 ml. Dry White Wine
30 ml. Sparkling Water
40 ml. Blood Orange Juice
5 ml. Green Lime Juice
10 ml. Sprite

Directions:
Put the green lime juice with the blood orange juice and mix them in a shaker with a few ice cubes. Add the wine, spite and sprinkling water on top. Garnish the glass with a few oranges and strawberries.

Citrus Garden

Ingredients:
30 ml. White Wine
35 ml. Citrus Vodka
20 ml. Green Lime Juice
40 ml. Sparkling Water
10 ml. Blue Curacao

Directions:
Put the vodka, green lime juice and blue curacao in a shaker with a few ice cubes and mix them well. Add the white wine and sparkling water on top and mix them with a tablespoon. Garnish the glass with a few green limes and rosemary.

Green Lemonade

Ingredients:
45 ml. White Wine
30 ml. Green Lime Juice
20 ml. Apple Juice
10 ml. Watermelon Liqueur

Directions:
Put the watermelon liqueur and apple juice in a jar with crushed ice. Add the green lime juice and white wine on top. Garnish the glass with green lime and apple slices and some rosemary.

Roselyn

Ingredients:
30 ml. Rose Whine
20 ml. Gin
10 ml. Triple Sec
10 ml. Grenadine
40 ml. Sparkling Water

Directions:
Put the gin, triple sec and grenadine in a shaker with some ice cubes. Shake it well and add the sparkling water and rose wine on top. Put some apples and lemons in the glass.

Bad Blood

Ingredients:
30 ml. Red Wine
20 ml. Strawberry Vodka
10 ml. Green Lime Juice
40 ml. Orange Juice

Directions:
Put the vodka, orange juice and strawberry vodka in a shaker with some ice cubes. Add the red wine on top and mix it with a tablespoon.

Peach Wine

Ingredients:
40 ml. Dry White Wine
20 ml. Archers
35 ml. Peach Juice
20 ml. Sparkling Water

Directions:
Put all of the ingredients in a glass with a lot of ice, and garnish it with a few peach slices.

Red & Yellow

Ingredients:
30 ml. White Wine
20 ml. Vanilla Vodka
40 ml. Lemonade
40 ml. Sprite
+ Strawberries and lemons

Directions:
Put all of the ingredients in a glass with a lot of ice and mix everything with a tablespoon. Garnish the glass with some strawberries and lemons and rosemary.

Submarine

Ingredients:
40 ml. Red Wine
50 ml. Blueberry Soda
10 ml. Strawberry Syrup
20 ml. Grenadine

Directions:
Put grenadine and strawberry syrup in a shaker with a few ice cubes. Pour the liquids in a big glass and add the wine and blueberry soda on top. Garnish the glass with a few blueberries and strawberries.

Paradise Nectar

Ingredients:
35 ml. White Wine
45 ml. Mango nectar
20 ml. Apple Syrup
10 ml. Grenadine

Directions:
Mix the grenadine, apple syrup and mango nectar in a shaker with a few ice cubes. Put it in a long glass and add the wine.

Thunder Cry

Ingredients:
40 ml. White Wine
20 ml. Malibu
50 ml. Orange Juice

Directions:
Put the orange juice and Malibu in a shaker with a few ice cubes. Add the white wine on top and garnish the glass with few oranges.

Falling Sky

Ingredients:
40 ml. White Wine
20 ml. Raspberry Vodka
10 ml. Sweet & Sour
25 ml. Blue Curacao

Directions:
Put the raspberry vodka, sweet & sour and blue curacao in a shaker with a few ice cubes. Shake it and pour it in a martini glass. Add the blue curacao on top and mix it well with a tablespoon. Garnish the glass with sugar and cherries on a stick.

The Passenger

Ingredients
40 ml. White Wine
45 ml. Coca Cola
25 ml. Green Lime Juice
10 ml. Triple Sec

Directions:
Mix the triple sec with the green lime juice. Pour the liquids in a long glass and then add the coca cola and white wine on top. Garnish the glass with green lime and menthol leaves.

BEER COCKTAILS

Paradise Lost

Ingredients:
50 ml. Ginger Beer
20 ml. Dark Rum
20 ml. Lime Juice

Directions:
Combine all ingredients together and put them in a glass filled with ice. Mix with a tablespoon and garnish the glass with green lime.

Atlanta City

Ingredients:
50 ml. Light Beer
20 ml. Bacardi
30 ml. Red Orange Juice
30 ml. Guava Nectar

Directions:
Combine all ingredients together and put them in a glass filled with ice. Mix with a tablespoon and garnish the glass with red orange.

Karma

Ingredients:
30 ml. Light Beer
10 ml. Vodka
10 ml. Lemon Juice
10 ml. Raspberry syrup

Directions:
Combine all ingredients together and put them in a glass filled with ice. Mix with a tablespoon and garnish the glass with lemon and mint leaves.

Devious Lady

Ingredients:
40 ml. Dark Beer
20 ml. Cherry Syrup

Directions:
Combine these two ingredients together and put them in a glass filled with ice. Mix with a tablespoon and garnish the glass with some fruit.

Sensai

Ingredients:
50 ml. Light Beer
20 ml. Tangerine Juice
35 ml. Campari
10 ml. Grenadine

Directions:
Mix all ingredients together with a tablespoon and garnish the glass with some seasonal fruit.

Strange Man in the Rain

Ingredients:
30 ml. Non-alcohol beer
60 ml. Somersby Apple Cider
20 ml. Apple Liqueur

Directions:
Put all of the ingredients in a glass and mix them with a tablespoon. Garnish the glass with apple slices.

Pear Flavored Beer

Ingredients:
40 ml. Non- Alcoholic Beer
20 ml. Archers
60 ml. Somersby Pear Cider

Directions:
Put all of the ingredients in a glass and mix them with a tablespoon. Garnish the glass with pear slices or any seasonal fruit.

Dark Passenger's Drink

Ingredients:
70 ml. Light Beer
20 ml. Champagne
20 ml. Sweet & Sour

Directions:
Put all of the ingredients together in a long glass and mix it with a tablespoon. Garnish the glass with lemons.

Troublemaker

Ingredients:
60 ml. Light Beer
60 ml. BlackBerry Cider

Directions:
Put these two ingredients in a long glass with ice. Garnish the glass with any seasonal fruit.

Shadow Ally

Ingredients:
40 ml. Dark Beer
20 ml. Baileys
20 ml. Jameson Whiskey

Directions:
Mix all of the ingredients in a medium glass and garnish it with some seasonal fruit.

Summer in Brazil

Ingredients:
30 ml. Light Beer
60 ml. Somersby Cranberry
30 ml. Grenadine

Directions:
Put all of the ingredients in a long glass with a lot of ice. Garnish the glass with some seasonal fruit.

King of Jungle

Ingredients:
30 ml. Non-Alcoholic Beer
40 ml. Elderflower Somersby

Directions:
Put all two ingredients in a long glass with a lot of ice. Garnish the glass with some rosemary.

99 Nights

Ingredients:
30 ml. Non-Alcoholic Beer
30 ml. Watermelon syrup
20 ml. Grenadine

Directions:
Mix all of the ingredients together in a glass with a lot of ice. Garnish the glass with some seasonal fruit.

Rendez-Vouz

Ingredients:
30 ml. Non- Alcoholic Beer
30 ml. Strawberry Syrup
30 ml. Grenadine

Directions:
Mix all of the ingredients together in a glass filled with ice. Garnish the glass with some mint leaves.

Walking on the Sun

Ingredients:
40 ml. Light Beer
30 ml. Smirnoff Wild Grape
20 ml. Wild Grape Monin Syrup

Directions:
Mix all of the ingredients together in a glass filled with ice. Garnish the glass with some grapes and mint leaves.

Mi casa es tu casa

Ingredients:
30 ml. Light Beer
20 ml. Orange Syrup

Directions:
Mix these two ingredients together and put them in a long glass filled with ice. Garnish the glass with some oranges.

Tequila Beer

Ingredients:
60 ml. Light Beer
30 ml. White Tequila
20 ml. Strawberry Syrup

Directions:
Mix all of the ingredients together in a glass filled with ice. Garnish the glass with a strawberry.

Ginger Beer

Ingredients:
60 ml. Light Beer
30 ml. Ginger Syrup
30 ml. Grapefruit Syrup

Directions:
Mix all of the ingredients together in a glass filled with ice. Garnish the glass with a grapefruit peel.

Fruity Beer

Ingredients:
40 ml. Light Beer
30 ml. Le Fruit de Monin Syrup
40 ml. Orange Juice

Directions:
Put the syrup in the glass and then add beer and orange juice. Mix them with a tablespoon and garnish the glass with an orange slice.

Parachute Pass

Ingredients:
40 ml. Dark Beer
20 ml. Cherry Syrup
30 ml. Cherry Juice

Directions:
Mix these ingredients together in a glass and add cherry on top.

CHAMPAGNE COCKTAILS

Italian Sunset

Ingredients:
30 ml. Prosecco
40 ml. Orange Juice
30 ml. Cranberry Juice
15 ml. Grenadine

Directions:
Put prosecco, orange juice and cranberry juice in a glass filled with ice. Add the grenadine on top. Garnish the glass with some orange slices.

Peachy Champagne Cocktail

Ingredients:
45 ml. Champagne
10 ml. Archers
20 ml. Peach Syrup

Directions:
Mix the peach syrup and archers together in a shaker filled with ice. Add the champagne on top and serve it in a long glass. Garnish the glass with some lemons.

Fruity Champagne

Ingredients:
35 ml. Champagne
25 ml. Pineapple Juice
25ml. Mango Nectar

Directions:
Mix all of the ingredients in a long glass with a lot of ice. Garnish the glass with pineapple slice.

Fancy Champagne Lady

Ingredients:
45 ml. Champagne
10 ml. Fresh Lime Juice
35 ml. Lemonade Soda

Directions:
Mix all of the ingredients together in a long glass. Garnish the glass with some lemon slices and rosemary.

The Weekend

Ingredients:
45 ml. Champagne
20 ml. Khalua
10 ml. Bacardi

Directions:
Put all of the ingredients in a glass full with crushed ice. Mix it well with a tablespoon and garnish the glass with some seasonal fruit.

Strawberry Champagne

Ingredients:
35 ml. Champagne
20 ml. Cherry Liqueur
35 ml. Orange Juice

Directions:
Put everything in a glass full with crushed ice. Mix it well with a tablespoon and garnish the glass with some orange peel.

Vodka Champagne

Ingredients:
35 ml. Champagne
25 ml. Citrus Vodka
10 ml. Sweet & Sour
40 ml. Sprite

Directions:
Put all of the ingredients in a glass filled with ice. Mix it well with a tablespoon and garnish the glass with a few lemons and menthol leaves.

Sweet Champagne Water

Ingredients:
30 ml. Champagne
2 tablespoons of honey
20 ml. Dark Rum

Directions:
Put all of the ingredients in a glass filled with ice. Mix it well with a tablespoon and garnish the glass with a seasonal fruit.

Red Elegance

Ingredients:
35 ml. Champagne
40 ml. Mango Juice
10 ml. Cherry Syrup

Directions:
Mix all of the ingredients together in a long glass with a tablespoon. Garnish the glass with some seasonal fruit.

Cakey Champagne

Ingredients:
50 ml. Champagne
25 ml. Cake Vodka (Smirnoff)
20 ml. Baileys

Directions:
Add the champagne, cake vodka and baileys in a glass filled with crushed ice. Mix everything well with a tablespoon and garnish the glass with whipped cream and cocoa.

Blue Champagne

Ingredients:
35 ml. Champagne
35 mk. Kinky Blue Ginger
20 ml. Blue Curacao
10 ml. Sweet & Sour

Directions:
Mix all of the ingredients together in a big martini glass. Garnish the glass with white sugar and some cherries on a stick.

Purple Mermaid

Ingredients:
50 ml. Champagne
20 ml. Kinky Pink
25 ml. Kinky Blue
10 ml. Lemonade

Directions:
Mix all of the ingredients together with a tablespoon and serve it in a martini glass. Garnish the glass with lime circle.

Hypnotic

Ingredients:
40 ml. Champagne
25 ml. Hpnotiq
35 ml. Cranberry Juice

Directions:
Mix all of the ingredients together in a martini glass. Garnish the glass with some seasonal fruit.

Red Bull Champagne

Ingredients:
35 ml. Champagne
35 ml. Red Bull
25 ml. Desert Pear Syrup (Monin)

Directions:
Put all of the ingredients together in a long glass filled with ice.
Mix it all well with a tablespoon and garnish the glass with pear slice.

Bittersweet Champagne

Ingredients:
35 ml. Champagne
10 m. Gin
10 ml. Bacardi
25 ml. Citrus Syrup

Directions:
Put all of the ingredients in a glass filled with ice. Mix it all well with a tablespoon and garnish the glass with some seasonal fruit.

Moi & Toi

Ingredients:
40 ml. Champagne
25 ml. Guava Syrup
50 ml. Orange Juice
15 ml. Grenadine

Directions:
Put all of the ingredients (except for the grenadine) in a long glass along with a few ice cubes. Mix it all well with a tablespoon and pour the grenadine on top. Garnish the glass with a few orange slices.

Afternoon in Hawaii

Ingredients:
35 ml. Champagne
25 ml. Hawaiian Island Syrup (Monin)
35 ml. Pineapple Juice
10 ml. Dark Rum

Directions:
Mix all of the ingredients together with a tablespoon and put it in a medium glass. Garnish the glass with some pineapple slices.

Fresh Lavender

Ingredients:
35 ml. Champagne
20 ml. Lavender Syrup
40 ml. Blueberry Juice

Directions:
Mix all of the ingredients together with a lot of ice, and put it in a long glass. Garnish the glass with a few blueberries on stick.

Delux Champagne

Ingredients:
35 ml. Champagne
20 ml. Pear Syrup
25 ml. Somersby Pear Cider

Directions:
Mix all of the ingredients together and put them in a medium glass. Garnish the glass with some menthol leaves.

Cherry Pie Champagne

Ingredients:
30 ml. Champagne
10 ml. Cherry Syrup
10 ml. Orange Syrup
40 ml. Orange Juice

Directions:
Put all of the ingredients together in a long glass and mix it well with a tablespoon. Garnish the glass with some cherries and oranges.

BRANDY COCKTAILS

Lady Brandy Cocktail

Ingredients:
30 ml. Brandy
20 ml. Khalua
20 ml. Hazelnut Syrup
Whipped Cream

Directions:
Put all of the ingredients in a shaker filled with ice. Mix it all well and garnish the glass with a whipped cream and cocoa.

Metropolitan Cocktail

Ingredients:
35 ml. Brandy (Hennessy)
10 ml. Cognac
10 ml. Dry Vermouth
40 ml. Orange Juice

Directions:
Mix all of the ingredients together in a shaker filled with ice. Pour the liquids in a long glass and garnish it with some orange slices.

Adventurous

Ingredients:
35 ml. Brandy
10 ml. Crème de menthe
35 ml. Coca Cola
10 ml. Green Lime Juice

Directions:
Put all of the ingredients in a shaker filled with ice. Mix it all well and pour them in a small glass. Garnish it with green lime and menthol leaves.

Peach Brandy

Ingredients:
40 ml. Brandy
25 ml. Archers
45 ml. Peach Soda

Directions:
Mix all of the ingredients together in a long glass and garnish it with some peach slices.

Refreshing Raspberry Cocktail

Ingredients:
35 ml. E&J Brandy
25 ml. Raspberry Liqueur
10 ml. Blueberry Juice

Directions:
Mix all of the ingredients together in a long glass. Put some ice cubes and garnish the glass with raspberries.

Navy Cocktail

Ingredients:
35 ml. Brandy (Courvoisier)
25 ml. Blue Curacao
40 ml. Sprite

Directions:
Mix all of the ingredients together in a glass filled with ice. Garnish the glass with some lemon slices.

Apple Brandy

Ingredients:
35 ml. Brandy
20 ml. Apple Syrup
35 ml. Apple Juice

Directions:
Put all of the ingredients in a shaker filled with ice. Shake it well and then pour the liquids in a long martini glass. Garnish the glass with white sugar and apple slices.

Hot and Cold

Ingredients:
30 ml. Brandy (Remy Martin)
20 ml. Limoncello
10 ml. Sweet & Sour
1 tablespoon of honey

Directions:
Put all of the ingredients in a shaker filled with ice. Pour the liquids in a medium glass and garnish it with some lemon slices.

Ying and Yang

Ingredients:
35 ml. Brandy (Paul Masson)
25 ml. Pineapple Syrup
40 ml. Pineapple Juice

Directions:
Put all of the ingredients together in a shaker filled with ice. Pour the liquids in a long glass and garnish it with seasonal fruit on stick.

Headache

Ingredients:
30 ml. Brandy
10 ml. Whiskey
15 ml. Tequila
30 ml. Orange Juice
30 ml. Pineapple Juice
15 ml. Grenadine

Directions:
Mix all of the ingredients together in a shaker filled with ice. Pour it in a glass and garnish it with some orange or pineapple slices.

Clear Sky

Ingredients:
30 ml. Brandy (Mansions House)
20 ml. Vanilla Syrup
20 ml. Sparkling Water

Directions:
Mix all of the ingredients together in a long glass. Garnish it with some seasonal fruit.

Cranberry Brandy

Ingredients:
35 ml. Brandy
40 ml. Cranberry Juice
15 ml. Grenadine

Directions:
Mix all of the ingredients together in a shaker filled with ice. Put everything in a medium glass and garnish it with some seasonal fruit.

Red Brandy

Ingredients:
35 ml. Brandy
25 ml. Cherry Syrup
40 ml. Orange Juice

Directions:
Mix all of the ingredients in a shaker filled with ice. Pour the ingredients in a glass filled with crushed ice and garnish it with a cherry.

Sparkling Brandy

Ingredients:
35 ml. Brandy
40 ml. Somersby Cranberry
15 ml. Grenadine

Directions:
Mix all of the ingredients together in a long glass and put some menthol leaves and limes in the glass. Garnish it with a lime circle.

Delicious Mix

Ingredients:
35 ml. Brandy
25 ml. Pear Syrup
40 ml. Pear Juice

Directions:
Mix all of the ingredients together in a shaker filled with ice. Put it in a martini glass and garnish it with some apple slice.

Sugarish Brandy

Ingredients:
35 ml. Brandy
25 ml. Spiced Brown Sugar Syrup (Monin)
40 ml. Coca Cola

Directions:
Put all of the ingredients together in a medium glass and mix it with a tablespoon. Garnish the glass with some brown sugar and seasonal fruit.

Tropical Island

Ingredients:
35 ml. Brandy
20 ml. Tropical Blend Syrup (Monin)
40 ml. Tropical Nectar

Directions:
Put all of the ingredients together in a shaker with some ice cubes. Shake it well and garnish the glass with some fruit.

Summertime Sadness

Ingredients:
35 ml. Brandy
25 ml. Dark Rum
10 ml. Vodka
40 ml. Pineapple Juice

Directions:
Mix all of the ingredients together in a shaker filled with ice. Add the ingredients in a long glass and garnish it with pineapple slice.

Fast Drinker

Ingredients:
35 ml. Brandy
25 ml. Banana Liqueur
30 ml. Dark Rum
40 ml. Orange Juice

Directions:
Mix all of the ingredients together in a shaker filled with ice. Pour it in a glass and garnish it with banana peel.

20 and Over

Ingredients:
10 ml. Brandy
20 ml. Vodka
30 ml. Sweet & Sour
40 ml. Pineapple Juice

Directions:
Mix all of the ingredients together in a shaker with crushed ice. Put the ingredients in a long glass full with crushed ice. Garnish the glass with green apple slice.

Made in the USA
San Bernardino, CA
05 December 2018